Volume 1

FLUTE SOLOS
with piano accompaniment
Editor: Trevor Wye

INDEX

Chester Music

PREFACE TO VOLUME ONE

The short pieces in this volume have been selected for their tunefulness. They will all be found to be within the scope of a young player of limited experience.

These tunes have been taken almost entirely from the flute repertoire, and have only been transposed when the original key would prove too difficult for some players.

The keyboard parts have been arranged for simplicity both for teachers with a limited piano technique and for young players.

Breathing suggestions have been marked: those in brackets should only be taken if necessary, and will make redundant any slurs over notes between which they occur. Ornaments have been written out in full or simply explained in a footnote.

Trevor Wye. 1976.

NOTES

1. **Theme.   Peter Lichtenthal (1780-1853).**

   A doctor of medicine by profession, Lichtenthal was an active amateur composer and writer on music. Born in Austria, he later moved to Milan where he spent the rest of his life. This bright tune is taken from his *Theme and Variations*.

2. **Russian Melody.   Ferdinand Buchner (1825-1856).**

   The work of this prolific German composer of flute music is now largely forgotten. His *Fantasy* Op. 22 is the source of this haunting tune.

3. **Gavotte — Le Dédale (The Maze).   Michel Blavet (1700-1768).**

   Blavet enjoyed a considerable reputation in Paris as a flute player. This is a movement from No. 5 of his six sonatas Op. 2, which were published in 1732.

4. **Andante (from Sonata No. 3).   Antonio Vivaldi (1678-1741).**

   Vivaldi was a famous Italian violinist and composer whose enormous output covered almost every kind of instrumental and vocal music. The two Vivaldi pieces in this volume are taken from the six sonatas entitled *Il Pastor Fido* (The Faithful Shepherd), which were published in 1737 as Op. 13.

5. **Minuets I & II (from Sonata No. 1, K.10).**
   Wolfgang Amadeus Mozart (1756-1791).

   Mozart was a child prodigy who travelled extensively as a keyboard player. The six sonatas from which these two minuets were taken were written during a visit to England when the composer was eight years old. Originally for piano with violin or flute accompaniment, they were dedicated to Queen Charlotte and published in London as Op. 3 in 1765, at the expense of the composer's father, Leopold Mozart.

6. **Galliard.   Melchior Franck (1573-1639).**

   The German composer Melchior Franck held the post of Kapellmeister to the Duke of Coburg from 1603 until his death. His many arrangements of folksongs and dances for instrumental ensemble drew extensively on wide ranging European sources. Instrumental music of this period was very adaptable in that it could be performed by any suitable instrument or combination of instruments.

7. **Pastorale (from Sonata No. 4).   Antonio Vivaldi (1678-1741).**

   See note 4.

8. **Minuet (from Sonata No. 6).   Ernst Eichner (1740-1777).**

   Born in Mannheim, Eichner was a bassoon player who worked in Paris, London and Berlin. His compositions include six sonatas to be played by flute or oboe.

9. **Nel Cor Più.   Giovanni Paisiello (1740-1816).**

   The Italian Paisiello was one of the first composers of Opera Buffa (Comic Opera), a style which he helped to introduce to the court of Catherine the Great in St. Petersburg. Several of his many operas were performed at the court of Prince Esterhazy while Haydn was Director of Music there, and the opera from which this aria is taken, *La Molinara*, is one of those which Beethoven encountered while a viola player in the Opera House at Bonn. *Nel Cor Più* provided Beethoven with the theme for an early set of variations which he wrote in 1795.

10. **Intrada.   Melchior Franck (1573-1639).**

    See note 6.

11. **Nocturne.   Robert Nicholas Charles Bochsa (1789-1856).**

    Bochsa was the official harpist to Bonaparte and Louis XVIII. This melody is taken from his *Nocturne in F* Op. 50 No. 2 for harp and oboe.

12. **Siciliana (from Concertino in D).   John Baston (?-?).**

    Until the mid-eighteenth century, the term 'flute' meant recorder, but between 1730 and 1745, the German transverse flute became increasingly popular. The English composer John Baston wrote for both recorder and transverse flute. His set of six concertos from which this movement is taken was published in London in 1729 by one of Handel's publishers, John Walsh.

1
Theme

P. LICHTENTHAL

Andante ♩ = 126

rit. 2nd time

★ This turn is played in the same way as the written out turn in Bar 4.

2
Russian Melody

F. BUCHNER

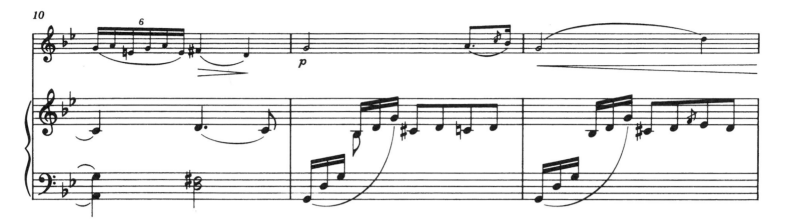

3
Gavotte –Le Dédale

M. BLAVET

~ is a mordent. It is like a short trill. Just let the finger bounce on the key as in playing the first three notes of a trill, though the first note *must be on the beat*.

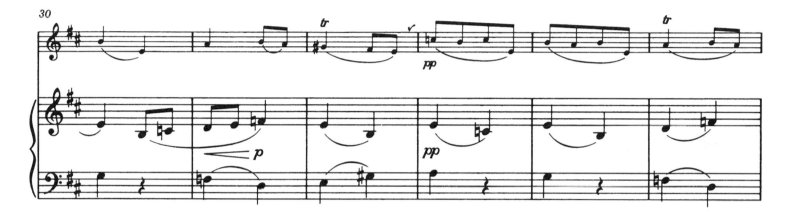

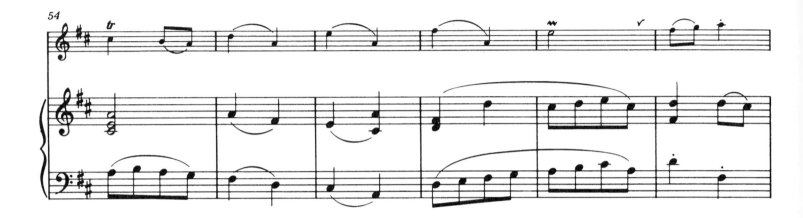

4
Andante from Sonata No. 3

A. VIVALDI

5
Minuets I & II from Sonata No. 1

W. A. MOZART

segue

II

Minuet I
Da Capo

6
Galliard

M. FRANCK

Minuet I
Da Capo

6
Galliard

M. FRANCK

1
Theme

P. LICHTENTHAL

* This turn is played in the same way as the written out turn in Bar 4.

2
Russian Melody

F. BUCHNER

© Copyright 1976, 1990 for all countries
Chester Music Ltd.

3

Gavotte – Le Dédale

M. BLAVET

★⌇ is a mordent. It is like a short trill. Just let the finger bounce on the key as in playing the first three notes of a trill, though the first note *must be on the beat*.

4
Andante from Sonata No. 3

A. VIVALDI

4

5
Minuets I & II from Sonata No. 1

W. A. MOZART

Minuet I
Da Capo

6
Galliard

M. FRANCK

All repeats 8ᵛᵃ ad lib.

7
Pastorale from Sonata No. 4

A. VIVALDI

8
Minuet from Sonata No. 6

E. EICHNER

9
Nel Cor Più

G. PAISIELLO

10
Intrada

M. FRANCK

11
Nocturne

R. BOCHSA

12
Siciliana from Concertino in D

J. BASTON

7
Pastorale from Sonata No. 4

A. VIVALDI

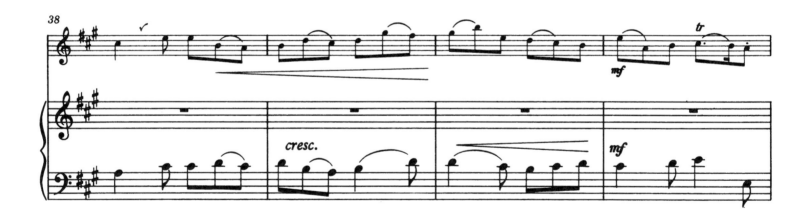

8
Minuet from Sonata No. 6

E. EICHNER

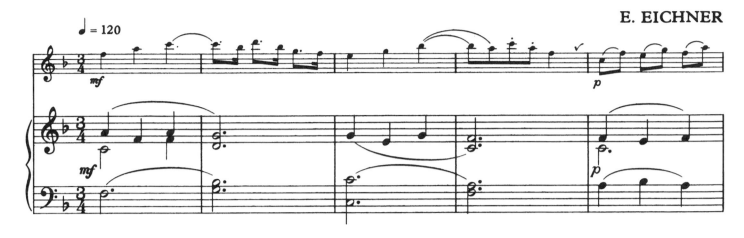

9
Nel Cor Più

G. PAISIELLO

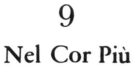

10
Intrada

M. FRANCK

All repeats 8va ad lib.

rit. 2nd time

11
Nocturne

R. BOCHSA

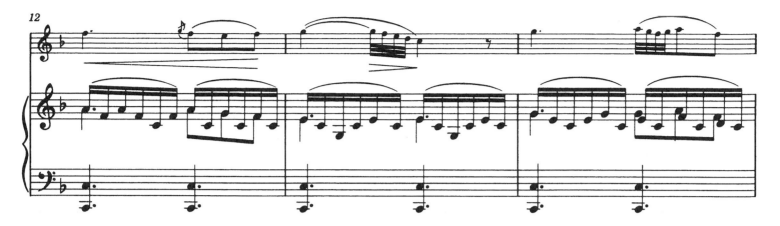

12
Siciliana from Concertino in D

J. BASTON

WOODWIND

Flute   Editor: Trevor Wye   Clarinet   Editor: Thea King

Oboe   Editor: James Brown   Bassoon   Editor: William Waterhouse

Saxophone   Editor: Paul Harvey

A growing collection of volumes from Chester Music, containing a
wide range of pieces from different periods.

FLUTE SOLOS VOLUME I

Baston	Siciliana from Concertino in D
Blavet	Gavotte—La Dédale
Bochsa	Nocturne
Buchner	Russian Melody from Fantasy op. 22
Eichner	Minuet from Sonata No. 6
Franck	Intrada
Franck	Galliard
Lichtenthal	Theme
Mozart	Minuets I & II from Sonata No. 1
Paisiello	Nel Cor Più
Vivaldi	Andante from Sonata No. 3 of The Faithful Shepherd
Vivaldi	Pastorale from Sonata No. 4 of The Faithful Shepherd

FLUTE SOLOS VOLUME II

Blavet	Les Tendres Badinages from Sonata No. 6
Chopin	A Rossini Theme
Donjon	Adagio Nobile
Eichner	Scherzando from Sonata No. 6
Harmston	Andante
Jacob	Cradle Song from Five Pieces for Harmonica and Piano
Mozart	Minuets I & II from Sonata No. 5
Mozart	Allegro from Sonata in G
Pauli	Capriccio
Telemann	Tempo Giusto from Sonata in D minor
Vivaldi	Allegro from Sonata No. 2 of The Faithful Shepherd

FLUTE SOLOS VOLUME III

Blavet	Sicilienne from Sonata No. 4
Blavet	Les Regrets from Sonata No. 5
Donjon	Offertoire op. 12
Eichner	Allegro from Sonata No. 6
Kelly	Jig from Serenade
Loeillet	Gavotte and Aria from Sonata No. 7
Nørgard	Andantino—Pastorale
Sibelius	Solo from Scaramouche op. 71
Telemann	Grave from Sonata in G minor
Vivaldi	Largo from Sonata No. 6 of The Faithful Shepherd

Also available: FLUTE DUETS AND TRIOS

Further details on request

Chester Music